MOOSE

Jack Ballard

FALCONGUIDES

GUILFORD, CONNECTICUT
HELENA, MONTANA
AN IMPRINT OF GLOBE PEQUOT PRESS

QL
737
.U55
B35
2014

To buy books in quantity for corporate use
or incentives, call **(800) 962-0973**
or e-mail **premiums@GlobePequot.com**.

MIX
Paper from
responsible sources
FSC® C005010
www.fsc.org

FalconGuides is an imprint of Globe Pequot Press.
Falcon, FalconGuides, and Outfit Your Mind are registered trademarks of
Morris Book Publishing, LLC.

Photos by Jack Ballard unless noted otherwise.

Project editor: Staci Zacharski
Text design: Sheryl P. Kober
Layout: Sue Murray

Library of Congress Cataloging-in-Publication Data is available on file.

ISBN 978-0-7627-8504-9

Printed in United States of America

10 9 8 7 6 5 4 3 2 1

Moose have occasionally been described as "having a face only a mother could love." This book is dedicated to the unwavering love of my own mother.

Contents

Contents

Chapter 6: Moose and Other Animals

Chapter 7: Moose and Humans

Acknowledgments

Special thanks for their assistance with this book are offered to two individuals. The first goes to Sarah Dewey, wildlife biologist at Grand Teton National Park in Wyoming. Sarah has been intimately involved with moose research. Her insights while reviewing the book were instrumental in helping the author revise several fine points. I also owe my sweetheart, Lisa, many thanks. She has self-lessly shared photos for this book (and others in this series) and offered numerous stylistic suggestions that greatly improved the manuscript.

Introduction

"Let's see how close we can get to those moose."

Not one to let a challenge pass, I eagerly accepted the invitation from my older brother. We were in our early twenties, hunting deer deep in Montana's Absaroka-Beartooth Wilderness. Moments earlier we'd spied four bull moose bedded at the edge of the timber, about a half-mile from our position.

When we crept from cover, a scant 150 yards from the bulls, eight moose eyes were already focused in our direction. Though I didn't realize it at the time, the animals' keen ears had doubtlessly detected our best sneaking. The moose didn't seem alarmed, so we strolled closer. At 50 yards it suddenly seemed too close. Just then, the largest member of the bachelor band rose to his feet, cocked his antlers in our direction, and snorted forcefully. The fact both of us were carrying rifles didn't matter. Our retreat was mirthless and hasty.

A couple of years later, while hiking in the same drainage, I happened upon a very large shed antler from a bull moose. In a lifetime of collecting a varied assortment of treasures from the wild, it is perhaps my most prized memento. It lay collecting dust in the garage for two decades. Struck with inspiration, I recently fashioned it into an elegant chandelier that now graces the table above a family retreat in New York's Adirondack Park.

Moose are fascinating creatures, both in appearance and behavior. At the present time, they're not thriving in the contiguous United States. Populations remain healthy in some areas and in the past decade have actually expanded in a few places. But across the board, moose are suffering. Populations have plummeted in states such as Minnesota and New Hampshire. More gradual but significant declines have occurred in the northern Rocky Mountains.

Are these decreases temporary setbacks in historically fluctuating numbers or the beginning of a serious downward spiral in American moose populations? More time and research are needed to answer that question. In the meantime, I hope this book will increase the reader's knowledge of this singular species and encourage a commitment to the conservation of moose.

CHAPTER 1

Names and Faces

Names and Visual Description

The moose is the largest antlered animal in North America. Bison are the only land animal on the continent that weigh more than moose. However, the average adult moose is as tall as a bison. Moose have very long legs. They exhibit a dark brown or black appearance overall, with lighter, grayish fur on the lower portions of their legs. The belly and inside of the legs are also grayish. On overcast days or in low light, the coat of some moose often looks very black. While their dominant coloration is similar, the coats of males and females differ in certain ways. Males have a very dark

The flap of skin below a moose's chin is called the "bell" or "dewlap" and is more pronounced on bulls than on cows.

muzzle, while the muzzle of a cow is medium or light brown. Both sexes have a short, stubby tail. Cows have a light patch of fur just below their tail. In the spring, prior to shedding their winter coat, the fur on moose may appear lighter and more faded than at other times of the year.

Viewed from the side, a moose is a lanky creature that may remind some people of a horse. Moose have a long face terminating in a somewhat bulbous snout. The upper lip of a moose overlaps noticeably with its lower lip. Their front shoulder is humped, while a curious flap of skin and hair dangles below their chin. The purpose of this strange appendage (if there is one), known as the "bell" or "dewlap," is unknown to biologists. The dewlap is larger and more easily spotted on mature males than on cows or young animals.

The term "moose" originates in the native Algonquian language of American Indians historically inhabiting the northeastern United States and southeastern Canada. In the native language, "moose" refers to these animals' habit of nibbling twigs and stripping bark from trees. Thus, the creature's name aptly captures its dominant eating habit in the native language. Linguists believe the term "moose" entered the English language from Algonquian very early in the seventeenth century. The scientific name for the moose is *Alces alces*.

Moose were confused with a related North American mammal, the elk, by early European immigrants. In Europe and Great Britain, the common name of the *Alces alces* species is "elk." In fact, the Latin term *alces*, whence the scientific name of the moose is derived, means elk. Early European settlers to North America may have never seen a Eurasian elk or moose (*Alces alces*), but they were aware of its existence as a large, antlered creature. When they arrived to the New World and encountered North American elk (*Cervus elephus*), they mistakenly named them for the Eurasian creature of the same name. Thus, the North American animal we know as the "moose" is commonly referred to as the "elk" in Europe.

Related Species in North America

The moose is the largest member of the deer family, a group of antlered animals with cloven hooves. Due to their massive size and unique color, competent observers are unlikely to mistake a moose for any other member of the deer family, although elk hunters have been known to accidentally shoot moose, thinking they are elk. Moose are much taller than elk, usually standing a foot or more higher at the front shoulder. While moose have an overall dark brown or blackish appearance, elk are tawny or light brown across most of their body, with darker brown fur on their neck and head and a prominent yellow or tannish colored rump. The face of an elk is noticeably shorter than that of a moose. An elk's muzzle tapers to a slender nose and mouth, while the nose of a moose appears round and bulging.

Elk are tan or reddish brown in color compared with the darker moose. Bull elk also lack the palm-shaped antlers found on moose.

Unlike moose, caribou have a white neck and mane. Caribou are much smaller than moose, and their antlers are shaped differently. SHUTTERSTOCK

In Canada and Alaska, moose sometimes share range with another member of the deer family, the caribou. Moose are huge compared to caribou, with adult specimens of corresponding genders weighing at least three times as much as a caribou. Caribou and moose are also notably different in appearance. While moose are uniformly dark brown or black over most of their body, caribou have a mottled gray or grayish-brown look, with a white or light gray neck that is unlike anything seen on a moose. Caribou also have a longer tail than that of a moose, which is white on its underside.

Two other members of the deer family also share the moose's range in many parts of the contiguous United States and Canada. Both whitetail deer and mule deer are frequently found in

Moose sometimes share range with mule (above) and whitetail deer (below) but are much larger and colored differently than either species.

proximity to moose. However, it's unlikely that even a novice observer would mistake either of these species for a moose. Both are much smaller than moose and colored very differently. Mule deer are predominantly gray in the fall and winter, with a reddish brown coat in the summer. Whitetail deer are brown or grayish brown in the winter, with a rich, reddish brown summer coat. Neither the size nor the overall color scheme of these species would create confusion with their larger cousin, the moose.

From a distance, bison might be mistaken for moose. Bison are large, brown herbivores (plant-eating creatures) whose height at the front shoulder is similar to moose. However, the characteristic shapes of bison and moose are dissimilar. An animal that primarily eat grass, the massive head of a bison is carried below its front shoulder. By contrast, the head of a moose protrudes above

Moose may appear similar to bison from a distance, but unlike moose, bison have horns and a much more massive head. LISA DENSMORE

its shoulder. The muzzle of a bison is short and broad in relation to its head, while the muzzle of a moose is elongated. The short ears of a bison are found on the sides of its head, while the ears of a moose sprout from the top of its head. Moose have an overall tall, long-limbed appearance. Bison look more massive. Finally, both sexes of bison have short, curved horns. Male moose have antlers that are much longer and shaped differently than the horns of a bison. Cow moose have neither horns nor antlers.

Subspecies of Moose

Biologists speculate that moose arrived to the North American continent from Asia via the Bering land bridge 11,000 to 14,000 years ago. As such, they are a fairly recent addition to the continent's spectrum of wildlife. How moose moved from Alaska, where they first colonized after their arrival, to other parts of North America is a matter of debate. Some biologists speculate that animals scattered slowly from the seed population in Alaska. Others believe small numbers of moose expanded their range in long-distance dispersals, creating isolated populations in suitable habitats that were far from the nuclear population.

A term of biological classification, "subspecies" refers to distinct populations within a species that exhibit differing physical characteristics or behaviors from other members of the species. Subspecies most often develop as a result of geographic isolation. Mountain ranges, deserts, and oceans are among the geographical features that may keep populations within a species isolated from one another. In addition to natural geography, alterations to habitat by humans may further isolate population segments within a species. Fenced highways, for example, may create barriers that keep animals separate. Large tracts of land cleared for farming may also effectively isolate populations of forest-dwelling animals from each other.

Historically, moose roamed across northern Europe and northern Asia in addition to North America. Currently, four subspecies of moose are commonly recognized in Europe and Asia, although a few biologists believe Eurasian moose should be considered a separate species from North American moose. Four subspecies of moose also inhabit North America.

The largest subspecies of moose in North America is the Alaska moose (*Alces alces gigas*), sometimes known as the Yukon moose. This subspecies is found in northwestern Canada and Alaska. Generally speaking, mammals found in northern climates are larger than their southern counterparts. Such is the case with the Alaska moose. Massive bulls of this subspecies may weigh as much as 1,800 pounds and carry antlers spanning more than 6 feet wide. A bull moose of this subspecies killed by a hunter at Redoubt Bay, Alaska, in 1958 had antlers that measured 80 inches wide. Interestingly, moose of this subspecies in their northernmost distribution are not the largest. Animals found at around 65 degrees latitude (N) in Alaska and the Yukon are the largest, with

Alaska moose, like this bull in Denali National Park, have the largest bodies and antlers of any subspecies in North America. SHUTTERSTOCK

body size diminishing in animals found north of 70 degrees latitude (N). Severe winters and poorer food sources likely account for the decreasing size of Alaska moose found at the northern extremes of their range. Some observers believe members of this subspecies have coats that are darker (nearly black) compared to other North America subspecies.

A second subspecies of North American moose exists in much of the interior of Canada and portions of North Dakota, Minnesota, northern Wisconsin, and the Upper Peninsula of Michigan. Known as northwestern moose or western moose (*Alces alces andersoni*), this subspecies was proposed by a Canadian biologist in 1950. The scientific name of the subspecies, *andersoni*, was given in honor of Dr. Rudolph M. Anderson, an eminent Canadian zoologist and explorer. Northwestern moose are typically not as large of body or antler as their Alaska counterparts. Nonetheless, they are ponderous creatures, with some bulls carrying antlers spanning up to 70 inches. Some naturalists note that northwestern moose are slightly lighter in color than Alaska moose, with the body appearing more consistently deep brown than black.

A third subspecies of moose, the eastern moose (*Alces alces americana*), ranges across eastern Canada and the northeastern United States. Eastern states harboring this subspecies include Maine, Vermont, New Hampshire, Rhode Island, Massachusetts, Connecticut, and New York. Dispersals of moose from Maine, which holds large tracts of excellent moose habitat, are largely responsible for the growing moose populations in other northeastern states. Eastern moose aren't as large on average as those found in western Canada and Alaska. Nonetheless, they can grow to impressive size. In 1982, a hunter in Maine killed a moose that weighed 1,330 pounds after being field-dressed (gutted) by the hunter. State wildlife officials estimated that the animal had a live weight of 1,700 pounds. A Maine moose shot by a hunter in 1997 (which became the state record-holder for the largest antlers) sported antlers spanning over 60 inches.

The final subspecies of moose in North America is the Shiras moose (*Alces alces shirasi*). These moose are found in the northern

Rocky Mountains of the United States, with populations occurring in Oregon, Washington, Idaho, Montana, Wyoming, Colorado, and Utah. The range of Shiras moose also extends slightly north into southern Alberta and British Columbia. In an odd twist of biology, the name for this subspecies traces to a Pennsylvania politician. George Shiras III served in the US House of Representatives from 1903 to 1905. He was elected from Pennsylvania's 29th congressional district. Shiras was an avid and pioneering photographer and was keenly interested in wildlife biology, particularly moose. In 1935 he published a volume of wildlife photographs that perhaps included the first wildlife photos lit with a flash. When E. W. Nelson of the US Bureau of Biological Surveys named this subspecies in 1914, he dubbed them in honor of his friend George Shiras.

Shiras moose are found in the Rocky Mountains. Bulls, like this one in Grand Teton National Park, may weigh over 1,000 pounds. SHUTTERSTOCK

Shiras moose are the smallest subspecies in North America, both in terms of body weight and antler size. A few extraordinary bulls have been recorded with antlers spanning over 60 inches. Male Shiras moose are sometimes described as weighing up to 1,400 pounds. However, any Shiras bull weighing over 1,000 pounds is an exceptionally large animal. Naturalists sometimes note that Shiras moose often exhibit lighter coloration along their backs that is lacking in the other North American subspecies.

Physical Characteristics

Unlike some small ungulates that appear much taller than they actually are, the perception of moose as a tall animal is very accurate. A mature Alaska moose male may easily measure 7 feet tall at the top of its front shoulders and weigh 1,300 pounds.

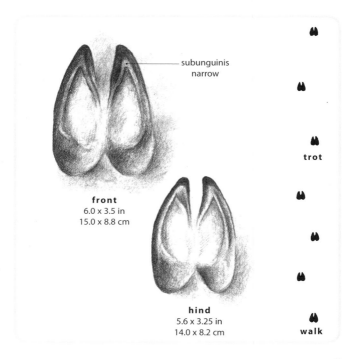

subunguinis
narrow

front
6.0 x 3.5 in
15.0 x 8.8 cm

hind
5.6 x 3.25 in
14.0 x 8.2 cm

trot

walk

ISSUES AND MOOSE

MAINE'S SPECTER MOOSE

From the late 1880s until 1938, an immense bull moose of mythic proportions and possessed of near supernatural powers was reported in the area of Lobster Lake, Maine. The animal was probably first reported around 1889 and was reputed as being 15 feet tall with antlers 10 feet wide. Two brothers, both expert hunters and uncommonly good marksmen, said they shot at the bull and both missed. Incredulous that they could miss such a large animal, they fled the area, believing the bull had mythical powers.

Subsequent accounts claimed the bull was white or nearly white in color. The animal's antlers were sometimes estimated as being up to 12 feet wide. Several hunters in the 1890s and early 1900s claimed to have hit the moose with bullets fired from their rifles, but none could kill the animal. One gentleman claimed to have been chased from a road by the moose while riding his bicycle, obtaining refuge from the ferocious animal after climbing a tree near the road. Stories of the behemoth moose occasionally surfaced in local newspapers and those found as far away as Indiana for a period of around three decades.

Exceptionally large Alaska males may stand 8 feet tall at the shoulder. These outsize males may also span 9 feet in length from the tip of their nose to their stubby tail. By contrast, the average Shiras male in Utah weighs less than 750 pounds and stands shorter than 6 feet at the shoulder. Moose exhibit considerable variation in size between males and females (sexual dimorphism), with mature females being 30 percent to 50 percent smaller than corresponding males.

Nomenclature for species within the deer family follows one of two patterns. Mule deer, for example, are named "buck" for an

While the reported experiences of humans with what is known in some circles as the "Specter Moose of Lobster Lake" seem on the far side of fanciful, the coloration of this mythical beast could certainly be real. Albinos, animals lacking pigmentation in their skin and hair, are occasionally born to many mammal species. In several species of the deer family, including moose, animals are sometimes born that have varying amounts of white hair but normal skin pigmentation. These creatures may be completely white in color but have dark eyes and noses. Commonly called "albinos," they are not albino animals in the scientific sense but members of a species displaying rare, recessive genes for hair color. Significant numbers of whitetail deer in some areas are white or mottled in brown and white pelage. In these places, more animals appear to be carrying the odd genes. The same pattern exists to some degree in moose populations. Moose with white coats have been photographed and rarely killed by hunters. Although the size and bulletproof characteristics of Maine's "Mythic Moose" are clearly fictional, his ghostly white appearance could be rooted in reality.

adult male, "doe" for an adult female, and "fawn" for an immature animal less than a year old. Elk and moose follow a slightly different scheme of identity for the various genders and ages. An adult moose is called a "bull." An adult female is referred to as a "cow." A youngster less than a year old is dubbed a "calf."

Moose calves typically weigh 25 to 40 pounds at birth. In contrast to the young of elk and deer, which are covered with distinct white or creamy spots at birth, moose calves are uniform in color. They look like a cute, cuddly version of an adult moose with fur that is reddish brown and much lighter than that found on

Female moose are known as "cows" and do not have antlers. Baby moose are called "calves." SHUTTERSTOCK

an adult. Maximum life expectancy of moose in the wild is about fifteen years, although they may live longer in areas containing ideal habitat with few predators. Several studies have found that cow moose, even in populations that aren't hunted, have a slightly longer life expectancy than bulls. Occasionally cow moose live to over twenty years in the wild.

Antlers and Antler Development

Bull moose have the largest antlers of any animal in North America, or the world for that matter. The weight of a pair of moose antlers can easily exceed 30 pounds for all subspecies. Moose found in Alaska and Canada may have antlers that weigh more than 70 pounds, with exceptionally large specimens achieving even greater weight. In 2012, a 73-year-old hunter in Alaska killed a gargantuan bull moose in the Brooks Range that weighed over 1,500 pounds. Its antlers spanned 73 inches in width, and were reported as weighing 98 pounds.

Carrying an extra thirty to 75 pounds of body weight on the top of an animal's head requires a notably strong neck. The neck muscles of bull moose are very thick and highly developed. Their antlers are sometimes used to ward off the attacks of predators and become potentially lethal weapons in battles with other bulls during the mating season. Not only must the neck muscles carry the antlers, they're also required to pivot and propel these bony weapons with great speed and dexterity.

Moose antlers are composed of bone. They begin to grow in the spring or early summer, with the antlers of older bulls starting their development the earliest. Bull moose have two bony protrusions on their skulls known as "pedicles." The pedicles are located on the top of the head, above and slightly behind the eyes but in front of the ears. Pedicles are slightly cupped and covered with skin. They are the "roots" from which antlers grow.

Growing antlers are called "velvet antlers" for their fuzzy, velvety appearance. The skin covering the developing antlers is filled with an extensive system of blood vessels that provides nutrients. Rapidly growing moose antlers can increase over an inch per day. The blood supply to the antlers decreases in late summer, due to hormonal changes. At this time the antlers solidify as bone and the velvet skin covering starts to dry. The "velvet" then sloughs from the antlers, a process that is often aided by the moose rubbing its antlers on trees and shrubs. Antlers are naturally colored white, but they take on various shades of light brown or reddish brown. The coloration comes from staining by foreign materials when bulls rub their antlers. Variations in the hue and depth of antler color depend on what a bull rubs his antlers upon, and how much he rubs.

Developing moose antlers require an incredible amount of energy and minerals. The energy required by a massive bull to grow 70 pounds of antler is notably higher than that required by

Growing moose antlers are covered with a fuzzy skin known as "velvet." Bulls achieve their largest antlers at around 9 years of age.

a cow to develop a 70-pound fetus. Phosphorous and calcium are two minerals used in great quantities in developing moose antlers. Researchers modeling mineral requirements for moose antler development in one study found that bulls whose antlers weighed more than 44 pounds could not obtain enough phosphorous from food sources and that antler development absorbed (robbed) some of this mineral from the animal's skeletal system. Bulls with racks weighing in excess of 66 pounds also diverted calcium from the skeletal system during a six-week period of maximum antler growth. Researchers have also found that bulls younger than 4 years of age have smaller antlers in relation to their body size than older bulls. Biologists theorize that while the bodies of bull moose are still growing, more nutrition is utilized for weight gain than antler development. Such seems to be the case. Researchers in Alaska have discovered that bull moose achieve their maximum weight at an average of 8 years of age. Their largest set of antlers is normally grown as a 9-year-old animal. Antler growth then tends to taper notably in animals exceeding 10 years of age.

CHAPTER 2 Range and Habitat

North American Range

The current range of many large mammals in North America is much smaller than the area the animals inhabited prior to European settlement of the continent. Elk and grizzly bears are two prime examples. Prior to the early 1800s, both species were abundant on prairie habitats east of the Rocky Mountains in places such as eastern Montana, and North and South Dakota. Overhunting and active persecution exterminated the animals in these areas. Current land-use practices and human population make it unlikely they will reclaim these historic habitats in any significant numbers.

Moose are common to the northern Rocky Mountains, although their populations have declined in some places such as Yellowstone National Park. SHUTTERSTOCK

Moose range in North America contracted as a result of overhunting and habitat loss in the eighteenth and nineteenth centuries. However, the loss of range was not as dramatic as that experienced by elk and grizzlies. Protection of moose with the legislation of hunting seasons in the nineteenth and early twentieth centuries and reclamation of habitat, accidental and intentional, allowed moose populations to increase and their range to expand in the past century.

Moose are currently found in most of Alaska except for the far western portion of the state. They range across most of Canada, with the exceptions of the arctic region, the southern prairies, and the extreme southwestern portion of British Columbia.

In the contiguous United States, moose habitat occurs in three areas: the Rocky Mountains, northern reaches of the upper Midwest, and northern New England. Moose range across northeastern Washington, with a small population also found in northeastern Oregon. They're residents of the mountains of eastern Idaho and western Montana. Moose inhabit the western mountains of Wyoming, with populations occurring farther east in the Bighorn Mountains in the northern part of the state and the Snowy Mountains in the south. Moose are also found in the northern reaches of Utah and Colorado. Scant historical records indicate that a breeding population of moose was probably never found in Colorado. Transient animals may have occasionally roamed the northern mountains of the state, most likely wandering south from Wyoming. Moose were introduced into western Colorado in 1978 and 1979 near Rand in two groups of twelve animals each from the Uinta Mountains in Utah and northwestern Wyoming. They have since expanded their range across the Continental Divide and are regularly seen in Rocky Mountain National Park west of the Continental Divide, with some animals pioneering on the east side of the park as well. Additional transplants in Colorado occurred in 1987, 1991, and 1992. Moose range is expected to expand in the future as animals move into the state's unoccupied but productive moose habitat. The Colorado moose population was estimated at 2,300 animals in 2013.

In the Midwest, moose range across portions of northeastern North Dakota and the woodlands of northern Minnesota. They occupy forested habitat in the northernmost reaches of Wisconsin and Michigan's Upper Peninsula. An isolated population of moose is also found on Isle Royale in Lake Superior.

Farther east, moose grace the woodlands of much of Maine. They also range across most of New Hampshire and Vermont in suitable habitats. Moose track forested areas in Massachusetts and have increased their habitation in northern New York. Absent from New York's sprawling Adirondack Park for decades, moose are now increasingly sighted by area residents and visitors.

Moose are abundant in Maine and have recently returned to New York's Adirondack Park.
SHUTTERSTOCK

The history of moose in the contiguous United States follows the same basic pattern of decline and recovery seen with other large mammals that had economic value in settlement times or were deemed pests. Early colonists happily killed moose for their meat and hides. Once abundant in the East with a range extending across all of New England and into northeastern Pennsylvania, moose populations declined precipitously, to the point it was believed only fifteen animals inhabited the entire state of New Hampshire in the mid-1800s. The situation repeated itself in the upper Midwest and the Rocky Mountains. Vast tracts of suitable moose habitat were lost to clearing for agriculture and logging, though timber harvest often improves forage for moose by stimulating the rapid growth of deciduous trees and shrubs. By the late 1800s, moose were found only in isolated pockets of their former range in the contiguous United States.

In most areas containing suitable habitat in the lower forty-eight states, moose numbers increased substantially from 1970 to 2000. However, moose populations in many regions experienced alarming declines from 2005 to 2013. In northeast Minnesota, for example, moose numbers dropped from an estimated 8,840 animals in 2006 to 2,760 in 2013. A full 35 percent reduction in the already compromised population occurred from 2012 to 2013, prompting state wildlife managers to suspend their moose hunting program. New Hampshire experienced a significant loss of moose during the same time period. In the five-year stretch ending in 2013, the state's moose number decreased to 4,500 from 7,500 animals. Total moose populations contracted significantly in stronghold states such as Montana and Wyoming during the same period as well. In a few areas, such as the eastern front of the Rocky Mountains in Montana, moose numbers increased slightly in the years that were so troublesome to the species in most of the United States. Biologists have yet to specifically identify the conditions that caused such a notable decline in moose country's moose population.

Moose Habitat

Moose are often classified as generalist browsers by biologists, meaning they receive most of their nutrition from the leaves, twigs, and bark of trees and shrubs. As such, they are primarily creatures of the forest. Over much of their northern range, moose are found in mixed timberlands containing both coniferous and deciduous species of trees. Although they prefer to forage in open areas or along the edges of timber, they routinely utilize heavier timber for escape cover from predators, for shade in the summer, and protection from severe weather in the winter.

Moose are creatures of the forest, relying on woodlands for food and shelter. SHUTTERSTOCK

Often found in the mountains, moose occupy a surprising range of elevation. In the Absaroka Mountains near my home in Montana, I've seen moose along lower-elevation creek bottoms at 5,000 feet above sea level to 9,500 feet, just below timberline, within the space of a few days. The mountains of eastern states aren't so lofty as those in the Rockies, but moose roam over a diverse range of elevations in the East as well. They can be found in the valleys or near the mountaintops, depending on the season and local conditions.

Shallow lakes and other water bodies often create excellent moose habitat. This cow and calf were photographed in Glacier National Park, Montana. SHUTTERSTOCK

Within generally treed areas, moose occupy various habitat niches. In many regions, the best moose forage is concentrated in small areas. Riparian zones (habitat found along waterways) are perennially favored by moose. Some of their favorite food sources grow abundantly along creeks, rivers, backwaters, and boggy areas. These include young aspens, poplars, birch, and several species of willows. A much smaller creature, unrelated to the moose, is responsible for creating ideal moose habitat in many places. When beavers construct dams, ponds and marshy areas are formed behind the impoundments. These provide water for deciduous shrubbery and may also stimulate the growth of aquatic plants, another food source favored by moose. Even after the beavers leave, old beaver dams often maintain a boggy area along the watercourse, which promotes good moose habitat.

In some areas of the country, shallow lakes and ponds also represent critical moose habitat. Lake waters less than 15 feet deep often support a profusion of aquatic vegetation during the summer months. These plants are often highly nutritious for moose. Aquatic vegetation growing in slowly moving streams may also be eaten by moose.

Within a given geographical area, moose occupy various habitat niches in relation to the season. In the spring and summer, they tend toward areas with easily accessed shrubs and trees that abundantly produce buds, flowers, and leaves. These may include subalpine shrublands, aquatic areas, and places that have been recently burned by a forest fire or cleared by logging operations. If it becomes very hot in late summer, moose will retreat to mature, dense forests for shade. They return to shrubby areas with readily available stands of shrubs and young trees in autumn and early winter. In mid to late winter, when snow depths are at their highest, moose prefer areas of coniferous forest with large trees that shelter them from the snow and cold.

SOCIAL TOLERANCE

While I was writing this book, a moose visited my yard in the wee hours of the morning. Ambling out the front door to let out the dog and enjoy my morning coffee on the front steps, I confronted a mass of leaves and small branches from an aspen tree strewn across the front yard. It appeared that a hailstorm had battered the tree in the night. Further examination revealed the tracks and scat of an adult moose and a large aspen tree with a very bedraggled appearance to its lower branches. Had the tree been younger, its value as a landscaping element may have been destroyed.

Not only are moose tough on landscaping in places where they take up suburban residence, they may pose threats to humans as well. Both cow and bull moose have been known to attack people, sometimes without provocation. Given the species' massive size and strength, a blow from a bull's antlers or a cow's flailing hooves can kill a person. Thus, moose make poor neighborhood residents where people are present.

Collisions between moose and vehicles pose another serious threat to humans (and moose) in some areas. A car that crashes into a deer crossing a highway may receive extensive damage. Imagine what happens when the same vehicle encounters an animal weighing five times as much as the deer. A moose collision typically causes extensive damage to the vehicle and may also result in serious injury to the occupants. Because the bulky body of a moose is supported over its long legs, the animals are often "undercut" by a passenger car, sliding across the hood and into the windshield.

The above factors usually make moose an unwelcome resident in habitat densely populated by people. Biologists often refer to this limiting factor in some animal's range as "social tolerance." Although moose could theoretically occupy habitats that provide sufficient forage and wintering cover in semi-urban areas, there may not be enough social tolerance to allow their presence. Thus, when evaluating potential moose habitat, biologists must access the social factors along with the biological.

Moose may move into urban areas where they damage landscaping and are considered pests. Urban moose may become dangerous to humans.

CHAPTER 3 Nutritional Requirements and Forage

Nutritional Requirements

The bulk of a moose's diet comes from browse, primarily the leaves, buds, twigs, and bark of deciduous trees and shrubs. An animal weighing in excess of 1,000 pounds requires a considerable amount of food to maintain its body. Moose are no exception. Biologists in eastern states note that healthy moose in the region typically consume 40 to 60 pounds of browse per day. At

Adult moose often eat 50 pounds of browse or more per day. This cow has cleaned most of the leaves from a tall shrub.

an average of 50 pounds per day, this means a moose will munch over nine tons of plant matter each year. The amount of forage available to moose and required for body maintenance varies considerably through the seasons. Research conducted in Alaska has indicated that moose can survive during the winter on just over 10 pounds of dry mass per day, but will ingest considerably more when it's available. The metabolism of moose slows considerably during the winter, allowing them to subsist on less forage than at other times of the year.

Nutritional requirements for moose also vary significantly in relation to an animal's position in its life cycle. As noted in the previous chapter, mature bulls invest considerable resources developing their massive antlers. Lactating cows (those producing milk for their young) also require much more nutrition than females that are not nursing a calf. Available nutrition is a very important component in the reproductive efficiency of moose. Cows with higher percentages of body fat in the fall are much more likely to produce twin calves than thinner females. Additionally, cows in better body condition birth larger, stronger calves than those that don't receive adequate nutrition.

Digestion

The digestive system of a moose is large, long, and complex. Moose, like deer, do not have teeth on the front portion of their upper jaw. They use the teeth on their lower jaw and their oversized upper lip to efficiently strip branches of their leaves or to nip twigs. The tongue and lips of moose are strong and covered in thick skin, allowing them to rake leaves from branches without the aid of upper front teeth.

Digestion begins when the animal swallows its meal of twigs, leaves, aquatic vegetation, or whatever else has captured its interest as a browser. While eating, a moose doesn't follow the human rule of chewing food thoroughly before swallowing. It simply rakes the forage into its mouth, grinds it a time or two with its rear molars, and swallows. The newly eaten forage lodges in the first chamber of a moose's stomach. It is later regurgitated and

The lips, tongue, and front teeth of moose are highly adapted to removing leaves and twigs from trees and shrubs. LISA DENSMORE

re-chewed by the animal, usually while lying at rest during the day. After it's swallowed a second time, the forage passes beyond the first chamber of the moose's stomach and into additional digestive chambers. From there it travels through the animal's intestines and is finally expelled as waste in the form of oval-shaped pellets. Moose feces (sometimes called "nuggets") are uniformly oval-shaped in the winter, having the general appearance of small eggs. In the summer, when the animals are eating primarily green plant matter, the pellets may clump together, sometimes looking more like cow patties than pellets.

Chewing plays a role in a moose's digestive process, but it's actually a complex mixture of bacteria and other microbes (known as microflora) in the animal's gut that is primarily responsible for

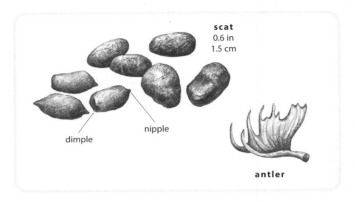

scat
0.6 in
1.5 cm

dimple

nipple

antler

digestion. Throughout much of the year, a moose eats large volumes of plant matter that have relatively low nutritional value. Its microflora breaks this material down into digestible nutrients. While the microflora works quite efficiently, it doesn't adapt quickly to change. During the summer, this digestive soup is optimized to handle moist, green forage. As summer fades into autumn, it becomes more specialized in breaking down woody browse.

Food Sources

In the fanciful children's tale *Thidwick the Big-Hearted Moose*, an accommodating bull moose allows a host of other creatures to take up residence in his antlers. When the rest of the moose herd abandons Thidwick and swims across a lake in search of more moose-moss to eat, Thidwick is left behind to fend for himself. The story has a dramatic and amusing ending, but Dr. Seuss, the author and graduate of Dartmouth College, either didn't know much about moose or didn't care if his story accurately reflected biology. For one thing, moose are seldom found in groups of more than a few animals except sometimes in winter and never in herds. Of all the things they might eat, moss is very low on the list. In a few locations, moose sometimes munch moss in the winter, but its normal contribution represents less than 1 percent of a moose's wintertime diet.

Willows are a preferred food source for moose in a wide range of habitats. This bull is browsing willows near Colorado's Rocky Mountain National Park.

Because they occupy such a wide range (Alaska to Maine) and are found in many different ecosystems, the plant species upon which moose normally browse may be very different in one region than another. However, certain types of trees and shrubs are eaten by moose wherever they're found. Among these, willows are one of the dominant species. Alaska moose are known to feed on at least twelve varieties of willow. In the northern Rocky Mountains, in places such as Grand Teton and Yellowstone National Parks in Wyoming, moose are strongly associated with stands of willows that grow along small creeks and rivers. One study of moose in Rocky Mountain National Park found that six species of willows composed 80 percent or more of their summer diet.

Along with willows, moose dine on the leaves and twigs of aspen trees over much of their range. They consume many other types of deciduous trees, some of the more common of which are cottonwoods, birch, maple, beech, and alder. Shrubs are another important source of browse for moose in some areas. Depending on the habitat, elderberries, currants, high-bush cranberries, gooseberry, buffalo berry, red osier dogwood, and mountain mahogany are among the shrubs often eaten by moose. In the Jackson, Wyoming area, they are often seen on sagebrush flats where they feed on bitterbrush. Moose occasionally eat twigs and needles from evergreen trees as well. These may include Pacific yew, subalpine fir, Douglas fir, lodgepole pine, and other species. Balsam fir, an evergreen common in the northeastern United States, is a staple browse for moose in many areas, particularly during severe

Moose eat a wide variety of aquatic plants. This young bull is feeding in the Madison River in Yellowstone National Park.

winters. Although moose consume a wide variety of forage that may include several dozen species of trees and shrubs, research in many different areas has found they typically focus on six or fewer key species at any given time of the year. For example, wildlife biologists in northern Minnesota have noted that 80 percent or more of a moose's diet comes from five or fewer plant species.

Browse composes the bulk of a moose's diet, but aquatic vegetation is a very important source of nutrition for these oversize ungulates in many locations. In the summer, aquatic plants grow quickly in shallow lakes and ponds, providing an abundant food source for moose. Slow-moving rivers also host various types of submerged vegetation, some of which are fed upon by moose. On several occasions, I've observed moose in Yellowstone National Park feeding on aquatic vegetation along lazy stretches of the Madison River near the park's west entrance.

The list of plants associated with aquatic environments eaten by moose is quite extensive. Along the edges of lakes and streams, and in marshy areas, moose may eat sedges or swamp grasses. These are grasslike plants with fibrous roots, often sporting distinct, triangular stems. In shallow water, moose target reedy plants such as bulrushes and cattails. They also eat bur-reeds, pondweeds, water lilies, and pond lilies, aquatic plants that commonly grow in water 1 foot to 3 feet deep. Aquatic plants rooted in deeper water, such as water shield and milfoil, are also relished by moose. Moose have been observed completely submerging themselves in search of these plants, and may remain underwater for more than thirty seconds at a time.

Why do moose spend so much effort to feed on aquatic plants? Similar to most other herbivores, moose love salt. Aquatic plants concentrate salt and other minerals, sometimes in astonishingly high quantities. Certain aquatic plants have sodium levels that are literally several hundred times higher than woody browse in the winter. Sodium and other minerals found in aquatic plants are important to healthy body functions in moose. Minerals and protein (also found in some aquatic plants in relatively high levels) are necessary for antler development. Sodium is required for

Aquatic plants are rich in minerals and protein, both necessary for maximal antler development in bull moose. Shutterstock

proper functioning of the nervous system. These minerals can be stored in a moose's body but are depleted during the winter, when the animals eat smaller amounts of woody forage with low mineral levels. Come spring and summer, moose are actively seeking mineral-rich sources of forage.

Forage Through the Seasons

A moose's diet varies considerably depending on the season. With the coming of spring, the animals encounter newly budding trees and shrubs, and the greening of grasses and broad-leafed plants at ground level. Moose eat the tender shoots of some grasses during this time and may also ingest broad-leafed plants (forbs) such as fireweed and dandelion. Newly emerging

Summer is the season that offers moose the most, and the largest, variety of food sources.

vegetation on trees and shrubs is an important source of spring-time nutrition as well.

Summer is a season of great bounty for the average moose. Leaves and new, tender growth on their favorite deciduous trees such as aspens, willows, cottonwoods, and birches are abundant. Summer also brings the season of maximal growth to aquatic plants. In many places inhabited by moose, beavers build dams of sticks and mud that impound small streams, creating ponds. Moose may find aquatic plants in the beaver pond and moisture-loving trees and bushes along their edges, making beaver ponds prime feeding areas for moose in the summer.

Green leaves turn to shades of red, yellow, and brown in autumn and eventually drop from the trees. Nonetheless, fall

Moose eat less during the winter than at other times of the year, subsisting mainly on woody browse. LISA DESMORE

HOW ABOUT A WINTER SNACK?

Severe winters with deep snow create a season of scarcity for moose. Witnessing an animal with sunken ribs and a hungry look, some people decide the moose needs to be fed and may scatter a bale of hay in its wintering area. Supplemental feeding efforts of this type do more harm than good. Because the microflora in its gut isn't prepared to handle a sudden infusion of rich, green feed, the hay may remain undigested and clog the animal's digestive system. In extreme cases, a moose may die from a belly full of hay or other supplemental feed of the wrong type in the winter. The transition from microflora that digests the woody browse that dominates a moose's winter diet to green forage takes weeks to accomplish and can't be shortcut. Many states, like Alaska, have laws prohibiting human feeding of wintering animals. These laws are not intended only to reduce potentially dangerous encounters between people and wildlife but, in the case of moose, to

normally provides plenty of food for a hungry moose. The small twigs sprouted by deciduous trees during the summer are easily cropped by moose in the fall and are quite nutritious. Moose may also find bushes loaded with berries, such as blackberries and raspberries. They're happy to strip both the leaves and berries from fruit-producing shrubs.

Winter is by far the leanest time of year for moose. Woody browse from deciduous trees makes up most of their diet across much of their range. Conifer needles and stems may also be eaten. During the winter the metabolism of a moose slows and its appetite is diminished. Research has shown that

protect the animals from misguided feeding attempts as well.

In the wild, one of a moose's final challenges during a particularly hard winter involves the transition from woody browse to green, succulent plant material. Animals sometimes die in the early spring, even though budding trees and emerging vegetation offer widespread and nutritious forage to a starving moose. If the animal's digestive system hasn't adapted to the new forage items, it may receive inadequate nutrition and succumb to starvation even as winter abates.

While the digestive systems of bears and other carnivores can adapt quickly to changing food sources, the digestive mechanisms of ruminants like moose, elk, and deer aren't so flexible. The ability to digest plant matter of low nutritional quality gives ruminants certain survival advantages. However, it also necessitates a gradual customization to new types of food, a process that can be temporarily stressful or even deadly in demanding circumstances.

even when moose have abundant, desirable food sources readily available in the winter, they still eat less than at other times during the year.

Migration

Moose don't undertake such spectacular migrations as some other ungulate species, such as herds of caribou and pronghorn. Nonetheless, they frequently move significant distances from summer to winter range. These migrations normally take them from higher-elevation summer habitat to wintering areas in the foothills or along lowland streams.

CHAPTER 4 Abilities and Behavior

Physical Abilities

Certain characteristics of moose offer hints of their physical ability, but their general appearance is anything but athletic. Their legs seem too long for their bodies. Their front shoulders are higher than their rump, giving them a somewhat off-balance appearance. The large, bulbous nose of the moose looks out of proportion to the rest of its body, and the dangling dewlap lends the animal an almost comical appearance, even if it's a massive bull with spreading antlers.

But like the gangly kid who becomes downright impressive the moment his sneakers hit the basketball floor, moose have many physical abilities that are nothing short of exceptional. Consider their speed. Moose can run 30 miles per hour or slightly faster. Their long legs allow them to navigate fallen logs and other obstacles in the forest while trotting at high speeds, a strategy they sometimes use to elude predators. While hiking in the Absaroka Mountains in Montana one fall, I startled a large bull moose. It whirled and dashed up a steep slope, clearing the yonder ridge and disappearing from sight as fast as a whitetail deer or elk. Compared to other North America ungulates, moose are very adept at running through moderately deep snow, an ability resulting from the length of their limbs. Their taller front shoulders make their front legs longer in relation to their rear legs, allowing them to more easily step over objects when walking or moving swiftly through thick timber.

Moose are also very skilled swimmers. They can swim at speeds up to 6 miles per hour and are reported to swim up to 2 hours at a time. Their swimming speed and endurance are promoted by their long legs and buoyant fur. The hairs that compose a moose's coat are hollow, which help them float. Moose are known to swim across large lakes or to islands in search of food.

The long legs of moose allow them to clear obstacles in the forest while moving at high speeds, one of the strategies they use to avoid predators.

Moose are very capable swimmers, sometimes swimming long distances across lakes or to islands in search of food. SHUTTERSTOCK

Although their swimming ability is known by most wildlife enthusiasts, it comes as a surprise to many people that moose can also dive. Moose sometimes dive below the surface of a lake to reach aquatic plants and can stay submerged for 30 to 50 seconds. The diving ability of moose, while real, is often exaggerated. Video footage has reliably shown that moose do attempt to dive. But due to their buoyant coats and air in their large lungs, they are not well adapted to diving, and their rear quarters tend to float as they dive. Some sources claim moose can dive up to 75 feet underwater, but these are certainly tall tales. Moose submerge themselves in search of aquatic vegetation, most types of which grow in water that is less than 15 feet deep. While feeding in shallower water, they often submerge their heads for similar periods of time, a bit like a grade-schooler bobbing for apples at a Halloween party. However, a moose is much more adept at underwater foraging than kids. Specialized tissues in its oversize nose create a seal that keeps water from entering its airway as it roots around underwater. Whether wading, swimming, diving, or foraging, the bodies of moose are well adapted to aquatic environments.

The senses of a moose are ideally matched to its woodland surroundings. It is commonly reported that moose have poor vision, but such a description depends upon what aspects of vision are most valued. Canines, such as domestic dogs and wolves, don't have nearly as keen eyesight as a human when it comes to differentiating colors or discerning detail. However, their eyes are much more adept at sensing motion. While the eyesight of moose doesn't appear to perform as well as that of canines or humans in relation to the above factors, their vision works well in other ways. The eyes of a moose contain many more rod cells in the retina than cone cells. Rods promote low-light vision and motion detection but do not allow for color distinction or clarity. Thus, moose probably perceive the world in shades of gray or have limited perception of color. They see well at night but don't have the ability to visually discern nearly as much detail as a human. Additionally, moose have a large "blind spot" in front of their head. This isn't a result of their poor eyesight but has to do with the position of their eyes on the head. The eyes of a moose are set on the sides of its head, which give it good peripheral vision but require it to rotate its eyes to see objects that are directly in front of it.

Moose have an excellent sense of smell, allowing them to pick up and discriminate scents at a considerable distance. Although little research has been done specifically to determine a moose's smelling ability, it's safe to say that certain odors can be detected from a mile away. The large, oddly shaped nose of the moose promotes its remarkable sense of smell. Moose have large nostrils located farther apart on the nose than the nostrils of other ungulates. Some biologists speculate that the oversize, widely spaced nostrils on a moose allow it to gather scent from a wider range than other creatures and may also create

The eyesight of moose excels in low-light conditions. The animals have a blind spot directly in front of them but have good peripheral vision.

stereo-olfaction, a fancy way of saying that moose may be able to detect the direction from which a scent originates much better than most other creatures.

Moose use their sense of smell to detect danger and also identify food sources. For people, the taste of food is related to smell and to the perceptions we receive from our taste buds. While moose have a much more highly developed sense of smell than humans, it's interesting to note that their tongues contain far fewer taste buds than a human's. It's quite possible moose select food items based primarily on their smell, not their taste. This may explain why moose will happily browse on the strong-tasting needles of evergreens in the winter, such as balsam fir.

Along with their keen sense of smell, moose also possess excellent hearing. Their large ears are roughly sixty times larger

Moose hear very well. Each ear can move independently. Lisa Densmore

than the ears of a human. Each ear can move independently of the other, making it possible for them to search for and locate sounds by manipulating their ears.

Like other mammals, certain senses of moose are more highly developed than others. Their eyesight is not as good as some other creatures, but in the forested environments they most commonly inhabit, sight distance is usually limited. However, their sharp senses of smell and hearing serve them very well. Due to these abilities, moose can often detect the presence of a predator long before it comes into view, giving them time to flee or prepare for an attack.

Vocal and Visual Communication

Compared to other North American ungulates such as elk, moose are very quiet animals. Elk communicate with each other in herds throughout the year with barking sounds and grunts. They become extremely vocal during the mating season, when bulls emit loud bugling noises and communication within cow herds increases due to mating activity. Moose, on the other hand, rarely vocalize, except during the breeding season. At that time, cows emit a very loud moaning noise that can be heard by bulls from up to 2 miles away. The call signals that a cow is ready for mating and is vigorously investigated by bulls. Some evidence indicates that cows may change the pitch of their calls when tended by young bulls. Some biologists believe this strategy is used to gain the attention of bigger, older bulls more fit for breeding, giving cows some ability to select their mates.

Bulls also vocalize during the mating season, emitting noisy bellows that alert cows and rival bulls of their presence. These calls are similar to a person making a drawn-out sound of a long "o" with a slightly guttural tone. Males may also make mating sounds that are sometimes described as barks or croaking sounds. At other times of the year, cows may grunt more quietly to call their calves. This grunt sounds like a person making an "errh" sound. It is somewhat similar to the moans and grunts cows make during the breeding season, but much quieter and

Moose do not vocalize as much as many other animals. Cows and calves sometimes communicate with grunts. Shutterstock

not as drawn out. Moose of both sexes sometimes make a very loud roaring sound when startled.

Although their vocalizations are infrequent during most times of the year, moose often communicate their intentions and internal state with body language. Cows may nuzzle and lick their calves, giving a visual indication of contentment and bonding. Bulls communicate dominance and aggression toward one another during the mating season by displaying their antlers and turning their heads. A moose that stops feeding to focus its eyes on a person or another object is communicating its alertness to a potential threat. Raised hackles and ears that are laid back are often preludes to a defensive or aggressive attack by a moose and may be used by both cows and bulls. Moose may also clack the

ANTLER AMPLIFIERS?

For some time, biologists have wondered if the huge, palmate antlers of a bull moose aid its hearing. Scientists theorized the antlers would gather and amplify sound waves. A pair of university researchers testing the hypothesis used the skull and very large antlers of a bull moose, which they hooked to a microphone on the skull between its antlers. The recorded volume of sounds was approximately 20 percent higher due to the amplification afforded by the antlers.

Some wildlife experts believe this may allow broad-antlered bulls to more easily detect the vocalizations of cows during the breeding season. Large-antlered bulls are more successful during the mating season, a factor some biologists think may be related to a superior sense of hearing. However, more research is required to clearly determine the role antler size might play in a bull moose's hearing ability.

teeth in their lower jaw against their upper gum just prior to violent behavior.

Herd Behavior

In many cases, the behavior of an animal species in one area provides a clue to its actions in another. Moose are the least vocal of the North American members of the deer family, giving some hint of their social structure as well. They do not form lasting herds and are seldom found in groups. However, moose do band together

Some biologists believe the antlers of a bull moose, like this one in Grand Teton National Park, amplify sound and improve their hearing. Shutterstock

at certain times of the year and under specific conditions. They congregate in varying numbers during the breeding season, most often when several bulls are attracted to a cow.

Bulls themselves sometimes form small "bachelor" groups. These are most often found in proximity to desirable habitat during the summer and early winter. One summer I observed and photographed four magnificent males near a lake on the east side of the Continental Divide, just south of Rocky Mountain National Park in Colorado. The bulls had taken up residence in a sprawling

Bull moose may temporarily congregate in small bands at various times during the year. Moose are found in herds only under special circumstances.

stand of willows, upon which they browsed vigorously. In such cases, the apparent companionship of the herd is probably more a matter of attraction to a particular resource than a desire to remain in the company of other animals.

A similar situation occurs during severe winters with deep snow. Several moose may assemble in a yard. The term "yard" refers to an area where ungulates mass together in the winter at a site of abundant feed. In addition to forage, moose have an advantage in a yard due to the trails created by multiple animals tracking through the snow, requiring less energy for locomotion. Once the winter has passed, the herd of moose observed in the yard quickly disperses.

CHAPTER 5 Reproduction and Young

The Mating Season

During the mating season, the normally quiet moose becomes loud and talkative. Bulls roar, cows moan, and both sexes communicate to each other with a variety of grunting sounds. What is the purpose of all this noise in a typically silent, solitary species? Along with other communication strategies, the vocalizations of moose during the mating season, or "rut," is what brings bulls and cows together, often from distances of more than a mile.

Scent is an important source of communication for moose during the breeding season. This bull is checking the smell of a nearby cow.

However, sound is not the only way moose advertise their presence to potential mates during the rut. Scent marking is another. While it's easy to assume that bulls do most of the searching for cows during the rut, cows are also attracted to dominant bulls. Male moose sometimes gouge the soil with their front hooves to create "rutting pits" or "wallows." They urinate in these pits and paw the smelly soil onto the underside of their belly or roll in it. Cows may also visit rutting pits and wallow about in them. Although the thought of this activity isn't so appealing to people, it appears to serve an important function in bringing together cows and bulls for mating. Moose may also rub their heads on saplings during the breeding season, another way of distributing their scent to other animals. Although biologists don't understand

The peak of the rut occurs in late September or early October. Bull moose travel many miles in the fall in search of cows. SHUTTERSTOCK

the exact ways in which the various types of scent marking stimulate the activities of moose, it is obviously an important method of communication between the two sexes during the rut.

The peak of the breeding season for moose normally occurs in late September to early October, although some slight differentiation exists in relation to geographic region. Small variations in the timing of the breeding season have also been documented from year to year in localized moose populations. However, in most places the vast majority of the cows will be bred in a short window of time, about two weeks. For example, one study in British Columbia found that nearly 90 percent of the cows that bore a calf the following spring became pregnant in a ten-day period. Cows that do not mate during the normal span of the rut may conceive

Velvet is rubbed from the antlers by male moose prior to the mating season, usually in late August. Shutterstock

calves later in the fall, sometimes as late as November. Although rutting behavior tends to taper off rather quickly around the middle of October, bulls may stay on the lookout for cows and remain quite aggressive for several more weeks.

For bulls, the mating season is a potentially risky and physiologically expensive time of the year. Preparation begins in late August, at which time the "velvet" covering dries and is rubbed from the antlers. Bull moose vigorously thrash their antlers against brush, saplings, and sometimes larger trees to rid them of the velvet. During the rut, antler rubbing also distributes a dominant male's scent.

As the breeding period of late September approaches, bulls become more aggressive toward one another. Confronted with a rival, males may turn sideways and circle one another, or tip their heads to display their antlers. As noted in Chapter 1, antler and body size are correlated in moose. Older males with larger antlers are generally also bigger and stronger of body. Younger males are intimidated by the bulky bodies and spreading antlers of these dominant males and will not challenge them for the breeding rights to a cow.

However, bulls of roughly equal size in terms of body weight and antlers sometimes engage in furious fights during the mating season. The conflict typically begins with the animals squaring off against each other and engaging in dominance displays. If neither disengages during the posturing, the encounter escalates with bluff charges and circling. The outright battle begins when the massive males clash their antlers together in a duel of strength, stamina, and agility. Protrusions (tines) on the outer portions of the antlers engage when the bulls begin their struggle. The combatants push and twist their heads in an attempt to reach the rival's ribs and flanks. If a bull is maneuvered sideways or loses his footing, he may be battered and gored by the pointed headgear of his adversary.

The winner of the battle claims breeding privileges to a cow or, in some cases, multiple females. However, he does so at a cost. Bulls in the prime of life (7 to 10 years of age) may lose

Bull moose may engage in furious battles during the breeding season. However, dominance is often settled at other times of the year when bulls test each other through more friendly sparring matches. SHUTTERSTOCK

250 pounds of body weight or more during the rut due to their increased exertion. In populations including a healthy number of mature males, biologists have estimated that the average bull receives as many as fifty puncture wounds while battling during the rut. Bulls sometimes suffer wounds that prove fatal during or shortly after combat. However, infected, festering puncture wounds that heal slowly and rob an animal of health as winter approaches are more common. In rare instances, the antler tines of fighting bulls may become interlocked in such a way that the animals cannot disengage them. Without human intervention, this unusual situation usually leads to the death of both animals.

Moose in diverse regions pursue different rutting strategies, a rather unusual occurrence among North American ungulates. In most places, cows maintain their solitary lifestyles during the breeding season. These single animals are sought by bulls who remain with the cow until mating, then move on in search of other females. In Alaska and the Yukon, however, where moose inhabit open tundra areas, as many as two dozen animals may assemble on rutting areas that are used year after year. Here, a dominant bull guards a group of cows (harem) from rivals and mates with them as each becomes ready for breeding. Even the most lordly bulls can seldom maintain a harem of more than eight or ten cows. If the harem contains a dozen cows or more, multiple males may be associated with a single band of females. The most

In most places, bull moose tend a single cow until she is ready to breed. Dominant bulls may sire a dozen or more offspring in a single year. SHUTTERSTOCK

reproductively successful bulls may mate with twenty or more cows in a single season.

Pregnancy and Gestation

The time from the beginning of pregnancy to birthing (gestation period) varies from 215 to 245 days for moose, with 230 days the most commonly reported average. Most moose cows birth their first calf at 3 years of age. However, cows reared in habitat with abundant forage may birth a calf as 2-year-olds. Cows achieve their maximum reproductive potential from 4 to 7 years of age, although in good habitat cows as old as 12 years may consistently produce offspring. Habitat quality plays a very important role in the reproductive capability of females. In poor conditions, conception rates (the percentage of cows that become pregnant during the breeding season) may be very low in cows older than 7 years of age. Where habitat provides abundant, nutritious forage, cows may produce calves much longer. Cows of at least 18 years of age are known to have produced offspring in the wild.

Some evidence indicates that the gestation period of moose varies in relation to factors that promote calf survival. Cows that breed after the peak of the rut may have a shorter gestation, which puts their birthing time on the later side but within the normal birthing period of other cows in the population. Females in less than optimal body condition may experience a longer gestation, which spreads the physical demand of pregnancy across a longer period of time and results in a larger, stronger calf at birth.

Birth

Moose normally birth their young from mid-May to mid-June, depending on the region in which they live. From year to year, however, there is little variation of peak birthing times in local populations. One research study in Alaska documented calving for a five-year period and found that the season of peak birthing varied only by about a week, even during years of notably different temperature and precipitation. The vast majority of births (80 percent or more) occurred in about a fifteen-day span.

Twin calves are commonly born to moose cows in healthy body condition. Shutterstock

Moose may produce a single calf, twins, and sometimes triplets. In good habitat, births may be almost equally divided between singles and twins. Twins may be completely absent or account for birthing rates as low as 0 percent and as high as 90 percent have been reported in various moose populations in North America. Cows tend to use established calving areas from year to year but birth their calves as solitary animals, not in herds. Birth weight varies considerably in relation to subspecies and other factors. The larger animals of Alaska and Canada birth bigger calves on average than their southern counterparts. Moose calves range from 24 to 40 pounds at birth. Cows receiving good nutrition during pregnancy have larger calves. Single offspring are usually about 20 percent heavier at birth than twins. However,

Moose calves are reddish brown at birth. They receive their adult coloration when their baby coat is shed at the end of their first summer. SHUTTERSTOCK

there is no significant difference in the birth weights of male and female calves.

Newborn calves can walk within hours of their birth and can swim proficiently within days. Their reddish tan color is noticeably lighter than the pelage of an adult moose, but beyond the difference in color, they look quite similar to their mothers.

Nurturing Calves to Adulthood

For the first two months of life, baby moose receive most of their nourishment from their mother's milk. Statistically, this is the most highly dangerous period in a moose's life. Mortality among infant moose is often very high. In areas with abundant predators such as grizzly bears, black bears, and wolves, as many as 75 percent of

PERMANENTLY LOCKED!

Although quite rare, the death of two bull moose occurring when their antlers lock during battle has been documented in many places. Typically one animal dies due to a broken neck, other trauma, or exhaustion. Unable to free itself from the burden of its expired rival, the second will also die if it is unable to disengage its antlers from the headgear of its adversary. In 2012 two dead bull moose were discovered in Wyoming shortly after a battle during the rut. Their antlers had locked. The neck of one bull was broken. His rival had succumbed to exhaustion, but when wildlife officials examined the carcasses they discovered the second bull's jaw had been broken in the fight, which would have eventually caused its death as well. The carcasses of bull moose with locked antlers have also been found in Alaska, Montana, Minnesota, Maine, and New Hampshire.

Perhaps the most famous set of locked moose antlers is now on display in New Hampshire. Known as the NH Locked Moose Antler Project, the display was spawned when the carcasses of two immense bull moose were found in Springfield, New Hampshire. The antlers of one animal measured an impressive 53 inches wide; the other's antlers spanned a remarkable 61 inches. Working together, several NH wildlife officials conceived, promoted, and produced a remarkable life-size re-creation of the bulls at the height of their battle. Featuring the full-body likenesses of the bulls mounted after days of painstaking work by a taxidermist, this artistic rendition of a real but rare occurrence in the life history of moose is displayed at various events and locations around New Hampshire.

baby moose may fall to predation in the first months of life. Those that survive grow rapidly, often increasing their body weight by 3 to 5 pounds per day. By autumn, most moose calves weigh 300 to 400 pounds.

Despite their size, young moose are still quite dependent upon their mothers during the first winter. They have yet to become adept at eluding or repelling predators and follow their mothers to wintering areas providing forage and shelter. Just prior to birthing her calf the following spring, the mother moose forcibly drives her yearling (1-year-old) offspring away. By this time, the young moose is ready to survive on its own but will often rejoin its mother and her newborn calf a few weeks after the young is born. Female moose reach physical maturity at around 3 to 4 years of age, but bulls may continue to increase in body mass until they are 8 or 9 years old.

Moose calves remain with their mother for their first winter. Cows lead their calves to productive wintering areas and buffer them from predators. SHUTTERSTOCK

CHAPTER 6 Moose and Other Animals

Moose and Other Ungulates

Moose share their North American range with a broad complement of other ungulates. At the northernmost reaches of their habitat in Alaska and Canada, they may be in the neighborhood of caribou. In the Rocky Mountains, they track much of the same territory as elk, mule deer, and whitetail deer, where they may also occasionally encounter bighorn sheep. Most eastern populations of moose have frequent contact with whitetail deer.

For the most part, other species of ungulates exert little influence on the lives of moose, but there are some exceptions. In the wintertime, moose may browse on shrubs and trees also consumed by deer and elk. However, it's likely that where overlap in winter browsing occurs between the species, moose hold the advantage. Due to their long legs and overall height, moose can browse trees and shrubs at heights up to 9 feet, far beyond the reach of elk and deer. Nonetheless, biologists have speculated that in areas holding very high concentrations of elk, such as Colorado's Rocky Mountain National Park, moose and elk might compete for winter browse. Willows are an important source of winter feed for existing elk in the area. Moose introduced into Colorado are now populating the park in rising numbers. Some biologists are concerned that the additional impact to willow stands of wintering moose may limit the winter forage available to one or both species. Research in Canada's Banff National Park indicates high elk populations may negatively impact food resources for moose. Because elk are less specialized in their diet, they may be able to outcompete moose, which utilize a narrower range of food sources in the winter.

Predation is a major source of mortality for moose in many areas. With the reintroduction of wolves to the western United States and their subsequent dispersal to other areas, biologists are observing a complex set of interactions between predators,

The relationship between moose and elk is complex in some places. Species such as willows are heavily used in the winter by both species.

their prey, and the ecosystems they inhabit. What happens when wolves move into an area containing high numbers of elk and much lower numbers of moose? While it seems the moose might be buffered from wolf predation due to the greater availability of elk, such is not the case. Research on predation to elk and moose by wolves colonizing Banff National Park in the latter decades of the twentieth century has told a different story. Wolf numbers in areas of abundant elk increase dramatically. Elk may constitute the majority of the wolves' prey, but due to their opportunistic nature as predators, they still kill moose, often in high numbers in relation to the population. Predator-prey relationships in regions containing multiple predators and several species of prey are multifaceted. Moose have direct relationships with other ungulates, but they are also associated with other hoofed mammals due to their shared role as prey.

Moose and Predators

The sheer size of an adult moose protects it from most potential predators. In North America, only two top predators, the grizzly bear and wolf, routinely prey upon adult moose. Many of their predation attempts on full-grown moose are unsuccessful. Moose can elude predators by trotting at high speeds through woodlands strewn with fallen logs, brush, and boulders, which their long legs carry them over more easily than the shorter limbs of a wolf or bear. Flight isn't the moose's only predator-avoiding strategy. Moose may elect to stand and fight, often choosing open areas or shallow water. These locations allow the animals to make the most of their long, powerful limbs. A blow from a moose's hoof can kill or maim a wolf and may even cause serious injury to a grizzly bear.

Young moose, however, are much easier targets for predators. Grizzly bears kill very high percentages of moose during their first month of life in many places, sometimes consuming over half of the annual moose crop. Wolves also prey upon significant numbers of moose calves in local areas. Black bears are another source of predation on baby moose, especially where wolves and grizzly bears are absent.

Although less frequent predators than grizzly bears or wolves, mountain lions (cougars) are also known to eat moose. One research project in Alberta, Canada, determined that moose are a very important prey animal for mountain lions in some places. In the study area, moose composed 12 percent of the winter diet for female cougars, while over 90 percent of the males' winter nutrition came from moose. The mountain lions preyed exclusively on sub-adult moose. Calves from 7 to 12 months of age composed 88 percent of their kills with the remainder targeted on yearlings, 13 to 20 months of age. Mountain lions in Utah have also preyed upon adult moose, although their threat to full-grown animals is usually very low. On rare occasions, coyotes may also kill newborn or young moose, although the extent to which coyotes can capably bring down moose is not well known. Nowhere in their North American range is coyote predation thought to be an important

Wolves and grizzly bears are the two North American predators that consistently prey upon moose. SHUTTERSTOCK

Deep, crusted snow makes travel difficult for moose and increases their susceptibility to predation. SHUTTERSTOCK

cause of moose mortality. If snow becomes deep and crusted in the winter, moose may be susceptible to predators unable to harm them in other conditions. The hooves of moose break through crusted snow, which impedes their movements, slowing their flight and tiring them quickly. The broad paws of predators like wolves and mountain lions allow them to run quickly on crusted snow, making it easier to bring down moose under such winter conditions.

Parasites and Diseases

Moose are indirectly but importantly related to other ungulates through predation. They are also affected by other ungulates in their roles as hosts of various parasites and diseases. White-tail deer in eastern North America are often hosts of meningeal worms or brainworms. These parasites exhibit a complex life cycle that takes them from a deer's brain, to its lungs, to its digestive tract, where they are finally expelled in the deer's feces. Tiny snails and slugs transport the parasites to vegetation, where they are ingested by deer (and other animals). Larval worms migrate from the deer's stomach to its spinal cord and back into the brain, where the cycle begins anew.

While deer are normally unaffected by brainworms, moose aren't so lucky. Moose, elk, mule deer, and caribou are all considered "aberrant hosts" to brainworms, meaning these creatures can become infected, but aren't the ideal hosts of such parasites. Infections of brainworms in these species are typically fatal. Thus, high numbers of whitetail deer carrying brainworms (in some areas at least 80 percent of the deer host the parasite) greatly increase the chances of moose becoming infected and may be

Brainworms, carried by whitetail deer, do not normally harm the deer but are usually fatal to moose.

a limiting factor in moose populations. Some research indicates that areas with very high whitetail deer densities (more than ten animals per square mile) are seldom inhabited by moose in significant numbers.

A similar situation exists between moose and mule deer in the northern Rocky Mountains, though probably on a smaller scale. In the early 1970s, researchers in Montana documented moose infected with arterial worms, a parasite that takes up residence in the blood vessels of its host. Mule deer are the common host to these arterial worms, but the parasites can also infect moose, elk, bighorn sheep, and whitetail deer. Recent research in Wyoming has discovered that high percentages of moose in some areas carry arterial worms. The parasite is transmitted from one species to another by horseflies, and it is believed a prevalence of horseflies may up the risk of transmission of the parasites. While Wyoming researchers discovered moose can live with some level of arterial worm infections, the parasites are known to cause the death of moose and possibly play a contributing role in other types of mortality. Concentrations of arterial worms can decrease blood flow to the head of an animal, leading to impaired vision, hearing, and brain functions. The extent to which arterial worms may be a limiting factor in local moose populations isn't clearly understood, but they may be significant.

Moose are also hosts to lungworms, a type of roundworm that inhabits an animal's lungs. It has been known for some time that moose may be hosts to lungworms, but the infections were seldom obviously harmful or fatal to the animals. However, more recent study has raised the concern that young or unhealthy moose infected with lungworms are more likely to die as a result of other parasitic infections, such as those caused by the winter tick (which will be discussed later in this chapter). Recent research in Maine has also discovered a new type of lungworm, commonly found in red deer and fallow deer in Sweden, is infecting moose. The degree to which this parasite may negatively influence moose populations is unknown, but some biologists believe it may be an important factor.

Other internal parasites also infect moose, with varying degrees of severity and harm to the animal. Moose can become intermediate hosts to hydatid worms (dog tapeworms), causing cysts in their lungs or other internal organs. Some research suggests that moose heavily infected with hydatid cysts are weakened and more susceptible to predation. Other internal parasites may also cause cysts in moose. Biologists have documented over twenty types of internal parasites capable of afflicting moose in North America.

External parasites such as ticks and flies can also be bothersome to moose. The most significant of these is the winter tick, or "moose tick." Winter ticks are frequently found on moose in the eastern United States and also occur in western populations. These parasites have a one-year life cycle that affects moose from

Severe winters can be beneficial to moose in the eastern United States by decreasing the number of winter ticks. SHUTTERSTOCK

autumn until spring. In late summer, larval ticks hatch from eggs on the ground and climb onto vegetation. They attach to moose and other hosts as the animals brush against shrubs, small trees, and tall grass. The tick larvae suck blood from the host, then remain dormant during the early winter. In January and February, the next stage of the tick's life cycle (the nymph) again feeds on the blood of its host. At this time the ticks enter the adult phase of their life cycle. The adult ticks again feed on the host around March and April. The ticks then mate and fall to the ground, where the females lay up to 3,000 eggs and then die.

ISSUES AND MOOSE

MOOSE AND CLIMATE CHANGE

Is the world, or portions of it, becoming warmer? While the magnitude and causes of global or continental warming trends may be debated, they will not be friendly toward moose. Warmer, shorter winters with shallow snowpack create more ideal conditions for winter ticks, an external parasite capable of killing moose and severely reducing reproduction. Cold, snowy winters mean fewer female ticks survive to lay eggs, giving moose a reprieve from these blood-sucking hordes of parasites.

Hotter summers create their own problems for moose, independently of parasites. The large bodies of moose do not dissipate heat very well. During torrid stretches of summer weather, the animals may simply hole up in the shade, refusing to eat. While this inactivity may not impact the survival of a moose itself, it almost certainly affects their reproduction. Cows that don't eat enough during the summer enter the fall with fewer fat reserves and may not breed. Females in optimal condition frequently birth twins; those with diminished reserves are more likely to produce a single calf. Thus, while moose may not be

Winter ticks can infest moose in such large numbers (up to 150,000 at a time) that they cause malnourishment and death. Severe outbreaks of winter ticks occur at various times and places in moose habitat in the eastern United State. Ticks directly drain moose of vitality by sucking their blood. They can also cause hair loss when moose rub their coats on objects in an attempt to rid themselves of the ticks. Moose with large areas of patchy fur due to heavy tick infestations have lost valuable insulation in addition to blood from the tick bites. Heavy winter tick infestations may also inhibit moose reproduction. Cows malnourished by ticks are

dying of heatstroke, their reproductive success may be compromised by climate change.

For many Americans, polar bears have become the "poster animal" of global warming. As research continues to unravel the complex lives of moose, it may prove that their health as a species in relation to climate change is equally challenging.

Climate change, in the form of increased average temperatures, may negatively impact the health and reproduction rates of cow moose. Sʜᴜᴛᴛᴇʀsᴛᴏᴄᴋ

in poorer condition and may not breed in the fall. Those that do are less likely to produce twins and may birth smaller, less vigorous offspring. Additionally, females in a reduced health state have fewer bodily resources to produce milk to nourish their calves.

Along with winter ticks, moose may be hosts to other ticks, flies, and mosquitos. While apparently bothersome, these pests appear to have minimal impacts on moose in comparison to pervasive infestations of winter ticks.

Moose are also susceptible to a variety of diseases common to other wild ungulates and sometimes domestic livestock. Epizootic hemorrhagic disease (EHD) and bluetongue (BTV) are closely related diseases carried by biting midges and sandflies. Moose in Utah have tested positive for both diseases, but their effects on moose have not been extensively studied. Infectious keratoconjunctivitis (pinkeye) has also been documented in moose in some places. This disease is most commonly associated with cattle and is normally contracted by close association with infected animals. Moose in the southern Rocky Mountains are known to occasionally become infected with pinkeye.

In addition to diseases caused by bacteria or viruses, moose can also contract white muscle disease. This condition is caused by a selenium or vitamin E deficiency and may cause excessive salivation, lameness, and heart failure. The extent to which it affects moose is not well known, but biologists in Utah have observed its presence.

CHAPTER 7

Moose and Humans

Moose and American Indians

Long before European settlers reached North America, native peoples hunted moose for their meat, hides, and antlers. Moose meat was an important source of nutrition for a variety of tribes in the northeastern United States. The meat was eaten on its own or mixed with fat and other ingredients to form pemmican, a portable food that formed a staple during the winter and times of travel. Some native peoples claimed that moose meat was more nutritious and would sustain a person in the midst of a journey much longer than the flesh of other creatures. Thomas Pennant, a biologist who lived in the 1700s, noted that Alaskan natives believed a traveler could cover three times the distance on a meal of moose than the meat of any other creature.

Along with the meat, moose hides were prized by many eastern tribes for clothing and moccasins. The skin of a moose is the largest and thickest of any animal found in the northeastern United States. Tanning (the process of converting an animal skin to leather) was very hard work. Tanning moose hides spanned several days of intense labor. Rawhide from moose skins was used to construct snowshoes, and Alaskan natives constructed canoes by covering a wooden framework with moose hides. Thomas Pennant also recorded indigenous peoples using the hair from the back and neck of moose in mattresses and saddles.

Large and impressive on a massive bull, moose antlers were used for practical and artistic purposes by native peoples. They were utilized for digging and fashioned into other tools. Pieces of antlers were sometimes carved to form decorative objects. Pennant documented native people creating ladles that could hold a full pint from moose antlers.

A handful of tribes had social societies named for the moose, and the animals appear in some native legends. But despite their importance to American Indians as a source of food and other

Moose antlers were used by American Indians to form tools and utensils. Shutterstock

products, moose were not afforded the same ceremonial or religious significance as some other creatures, including the grizzly bear, bison, raven, and coyote.

Moose were hunted using a variety of techniques depending on the region of the country and the season. Native hunters in areas where moose were relatively plentiful would use calls made of birch bark shaped like a cone to imitate the grunts of the animals during the mating season. This technique brought curious cows and bulls within range of the hunters' arrows. Some hunters also mimicked the calls of calves to lure protective cows. During the winter, hunters on snowshoes pursued moose in deep snow, easily overtaking animals when the snow developed a crust. Moose were opportunistically hunted in deep snow even in areas where their numbers were limited, such as northwestern Montana. Various tribes also set snares and devised deadfall traps capable of taking moose.

Moose and European Settlers

The history of moose in the United States parallels the fate of many other creatures. Where they were plentiful, moose were hunted by the colonists and settlers for their meat and hides. Elsewhere, moose were gladly killed as they were encountered as people went about their business hunting other creatures, prospecting, or ranching. Extensive clearing of woodlands for farming in the northeastern part of the country greatly reduced the amount of habitat available for moose and contributed to their declining numbers. By the end of the nineteenth century, moose range in what is now the contiguous United States had shrunk dramatically and the once common sight of a moose became a rare occurrence. In New Hampshire, for example, moose were plentiful prior to European colonization. By the mid-1800s their numbers had plummeted to an estimated fifteen animals.

Today moose are fairly common in the northern Rocky Mountains, in places like the mountains of Montana, Idaho, and

Journals from the Lewis and Clark expedition contain scant references to moose, although the corps traveled through excellent habitat on the rivers of Montana and Idaho. Shutterstock

Wyoming, although numbers there are far fewer than elk and deer. Unregulated hunting in the nineteenth century made moose quite scarce in these areas, but they were not plentiful prior to European exploration and settlement. The Lewis and Clark expedition traced routes across the northern Rockies taking them through hundreds of miles of productive moose habitat. However, their journals only contain two direct references to moose. In one, a hunter for the expedition wounded a moose on the return trip from the Pacific Ocean in western Montana, on July 7, 1806. The other journal entry is from five days earlier, and simply says Indians informed the expedition members there were "plenty of Moos" to the southeast of them (on the Salmon River in Idaho).

Across their historic range in the contiguous United States, moose numbers began to rebound substantially in the decades after World War II. A variety of factors led to growing moose populations. First, bans on unregulated hunting and the development of restrictive hunting (or no moose hunting at all) in many states buffered moose from a significant source of mortality. Maine's legacy with moose hunting is instructive at this point. In 1830, just ten years after Maine became a state, a law was passed setting the moose hunting season (with no bag limit) from September 1 to December 31. Further restrictions on the moose season were set by the 1883 legislature, shortening the moose season, enacting a possession limit of one moose, forbidding hunting on Sunday, and regulating hunting with dogs. The legislature also provided for strengthened enforcement of game laws. Several groups promoting ethical hunting and the preservation of natural resources became active in Maine in the late nineteenth century. Public support for wildlife conservation expanded, resulting in an 1891 law prohibiting the killing of cow and calf moose. Declining populations prompted the legislature to suspend moose hunting altogether in 1935. Maine did not reopen its moose hunting season until 1980. Since then, restrictive harvests have ensured hunting does not negatively impact the viability of local moose populations.

A similar pattern applied to moose management in other eastern states. New Hampshire, for example, opened a moose hunting season in 1988 after decades of strict moose protection. In the West, historical records of moose populations in the late nineteenth and early twentieth centuries are sketchy. However, it appears many populations actually expanded during these times. Moose are believed to have colonized Wyoming from Idaho and Montana around 150 years ago. In 1903 the Wyoming state legislature closed its moose hunt but reopened it in 1912 due to an expanding population estimated at 500 animals. Available data indicates moose fared better in the West than the East during the first half of the 1900s.

Protection from hunters ensured moose weren't being legally killed by humans. However, habitat enhancement was equally important to the moose population recovery in the West in the early decades of the twentieth century and in the East in the latter half of the twentieth century. Logging, wildfires, and changing land use all played a role.

Logging often promotes the growth of deciduous trees and shrubs in forested areas and is generally beneficial to moose. Shutterstock

In general, logging is beneficial to moose. Areas cleared of timber sprout deciduous trees and shrubs in prolific numbers when mature trees are eliminated, creating ideal browsing areas for moose. Where logging results in a mosaic of oases of mature timber interspersed with cleared areas in various states of recovery, moose find both excellent forage and sheltered wintering areas. Logging in the twentieth century in many regions of the country doubtlessly enhanced moose habitat.

Alterations in land use in the East also benefitted moose. Settlers cleared hundreds of thousands of acres in the New England states for farming, land that ultimately proved unsuitable for crops. As the pastures and fields were abandoned, they reverted to woodlands. Fast-growing deciduous shrub and trees were first to overrun the neglected fields, creating fine moose habitat in the process.

In the West, large-scale wildfires occurred in the early decades of the twentieth century. Fire activity again increased in the 1980s and 1990s. Management of fires on public lands has also

Forest fires are often instrumental in regenerating habitat. Moose may benefit from fires for several decades after the burn. SHUTTERSTOCK

undergone a shift in policy in the past several decades. Recognizing fire is often beneficial to wildlife habitat, land managers are more inclined to let some fires burn than attempt their immediate extinction. In some places, controlled fires are deliberately set to rejuvenate habitat. Burned areas often result in increased forage for moose in the form of leaf-bearing shrubs and trees. Sometimes the habitat enhancement occurs within a few years; in other places the maximum benefit for moose takes a couple of decades. In either case, fire activity in the West has typically been good for moose.

Moose and Us

The scientific study of moose has lagged behind the depth of research devoted to many other North American species. However, the current decline in many moose populations has prompted an increased interest in these unique creatures. Some experts believe the contemporary contraction of moose numbers is simply an episode in the long-term history of a species prone to intense fluctuations in population due to changing habitat conditions and other yet-to-be-identified variables. Other biologists are more concerned, believing lengthy variations in climate conditions (drought, warming) and exposure to increased predation may put pressure upon moose populations from which the animals are less likely to recover.

At a more practical level, it's helpful for modern humans to be aware of hazards to themselves and the animals when traveling in moose country. Collisions with vehicles are a significant source of mortality to moose in some areas, sometimes killing vehicle occupants and resulting in extensive damage to automobiles. In Alaska, around 500 moose-vehicle collisions are reported annually. Highway officials estimate that over 20 percent of vehicle accidents on rural roads in Alaska involve moose collisions, and can double during severe winters. The Alaska Department of Fish and Game believes the number of moose-vehicle collisions may actually be up to 15 percentage points higher, since accidents are often unreported. In New Hampshire, around 250 moose-vehicle

Vehicle collisions are a significant source of moose mortality in some areas, and may also injure or kill occupants of the vehicle. Sʜᴜᴛᴛᴇʀsᴛᴏᴄᴋ

collisions occur annually, with most happening around dawn and dusk from April to November.

Drivers can reduce the possibility of a moose collision in many ways. Slowing down increases the odds of avoiding a moose, and also decreases the severity of impact and the likelihood of sustaining serious injury in a collision. Driving with greater vigilance in moose country, especially at dawn and dusk, also helps. Moose are hard to see at night. Utilizing high-beam lights when possible makes the animals more visible. Some evidence indicates moose are attracted to roadside "salt pools" that remain after highways have been salted to eliminate ice in the winter. Moose may frequent salty roadsides in the spring to obtain minerals.

Humans in vehicles pose a threat to moose, but moose may also be dangerous to humans. Bulls can become very hostile during the mating season. Cows are highly protective of their calves. Both sexes are known to engage in unpredictable, aggressive behavior at all seasons of the year. Moose most frequently attack by flailing their front hooves at a perceived threat or opponent. A blow from a moose's hoof can crush a human's skull or easily break other bones. Most people fear grizzly bears, but the danger posed by a belligerent moose is no less serious than a riled bruin.

Giving moose a wide berth, viewing them from a distance, and making noise to alert them of your human presence are the simplest strategies to avoid conflict. Surprised at close range, moose sometimes give physical signals of impending aggression before charging. Raised hair on the neck and back, laid-back ears, and agitated snorting all indicate a moose is upset. Exiting the area as quickly as possible (at a dead run if necessary) is advised by many wildlife officials when confronted with an upset moose. If the moose charges and you can't escape, ducking behind a tree or climbing it are other effective evasive strategies.

Bull moose can be unpredictable and dangerous during the fall, and cows are very protective of their calves. Moose are best viewed from a distance and left alone. SHUTTERSTOCK

Moose can be dangerous and unpredictable, but most encounters with these creatures are quite the opposite. The opportunity to observe the behavior of this irreplaceable, intriguing member of the deer family is a real treat to wildlife enthusiasts. Whatever the future of these imposing creatures, human residents of North America inhabit a richer world in their presence.

ISSUES AND MOOSE

ZOO MOOSE?

Moose can be, and have been, domesticated. Tame moose have been broke to ride like horses and trained to pull carts and sleds. In bygone times, attempts to develop moose-mounted cavalry units were seriously discussed and experimented with on a limited basis in northern Europe and Russia. It was thought the animals would strike terror in the horses of opposing armies. Historical evidence indicates Tycho Brahe, an eminent Danish astronomer of the late sixteenth century, kept a pet moose. The moose was purportedly loaned to a nobleman for entertainment at a party. The moose consumed so much beer during the festivities that it became drunk and fell down the stone stairs of the castle, breaking a leg. Its injury eventually led to the creature's death.

Moose have been kept as pets in various locations in modern times, but you won't likely see one in a zoo. Hay and commercially produced feeds may keep the likes of elk and deer alive in an enclosure, but captive moose languish on such feeds. Their need for leaves, twigs, and fresh plant matter seems very important for their health, making them largely unsuitable as zoo animals.

Index

Index

About the Author

A writer, photographer, and naturalist, Jack Ballard is a frequent contributor to numerous regional and national publications. He has written hundreds of articles on wildlife and wildlife-related topics.

His photos have been published in numerous books (Smithsonian Press, Heinemann Library, etc.), calendars, and magazines. Jack has received multiple awards for his writing and photography from the Outdoor Writers Association of America and other professional organizations. He holds two master's degrees and is an accomplished public speaker, entertaining students, conference attendees, and recreation/conservation groups with his compelling narratives. When not wandering the backcountry, he hangs his hat in Red Lodge, Montana. See more of his work at jackballard.com.